Taking Off the Mask

by

Antoinette Jackson

RoseDog Books

PITTSBURGH, PENNSYLVANIA 15238

RoseDog Books
585 Alpha Drive
Suite 103
Pittsburgh, PA 15238
Visit our website at www.rosedogbookstore.com

ISBN: 978-1-4809-7638-2
eISBN: 978-1-4809-7661-0

2 Corinthians 4:8-10

We are pressed on every side by troubles, but we are not crushed. We are perplexed, but not driven to despair. We are hunted down, but never abandoned by God. We get knocked down, but we are not destroyed. Through suffering, our bodies continue to share in the death of Jesus so that the life of Jesus may also be seen in our bodies. (NLT)

Special Thanks

I would like to thank Sondra Schneider for all her help in making this dream a reality, and for believing in me. For the late hours, laughs, and tears you shared with me. For sharing my joy and sorrows and always ready to give timely help when I needed you most. Never asking for anything in return. You gave meaning to my life, and you complete it by offering a special type of relationship called Friendship. Thanks!!

Ms. Roselyn Knox, this thank you is long overdue. There many things I want to thank you for. This is just a token of my gratitude for just being by my side in this walk of life and making it all worthwhile. Thank you for accepting me and loving me for exactly who I am. For believing this book would come to be and never doubting. When I question whether I have "any good left," you're always there to reassure me and show me that I do. Thank you for loving me in the difficult moments and understanding me like no one else does.

Dedication:

I dedicate this book to the HOLY SPIRIT, the Revealer of TRUTH. He has shown me my true self and released me from great bondage.

Foreword

While sitting in the hospital waiting room one day, I met the most dynamic woman, Antoinette Jackson. She and I were attending, praying and poised for a miracle for a dear woman with whom we shared friendship. Antoinette and I danced the dance of new friends both wearing masks, however, our miracle came and the masks hit the ground!

You are about to be introduced, yourself, to the woman that I have had the honor to call friend and "sister." She has given herself completely to bearing raw truths and the secrets of her life to "unstick" women and other readers who are perhaps also painfully escaping intimacy, due to fear and embarrassment of past wounds. Antoinette has put herself on the line to share her most sensitive experiences. She hopes to show those with the strength to read her journey that no matter what our devastations are, we can survive, thrive, and finish on top!

Miracles are nothing new to Antoinette. She is a walking miracle herself. Inside you will uncover many, many stories of God lifting her from the pits to the "palace." You will find yourself realizing that you have much to count as personal blessings and your compassion for others increasing. (We will probably never again rush to prejudge our new "acquaintances.") People have worth and value. Antoinette's story reminds us to never assume that those around us are "okay" based on them telling us so. We must measure the heart not "judge the book by its cover." Her readers will come away with a sense of appreciation and respect for others and with a desire to always consider what those around us are possibly going through. Like her Savior, Antoinette reminds us to have compassion.

Until we can all be as truthful, we must seek for the courage to release what binds us. Antoinette's guidance has been her Heavenly Father. She would desire to guide you directly to His throne to begin your process. ("What He has done for others He can do for you", she reminds me!)

Don't wait! You will see that masks not only hide you, but keep you from your own peace and contentment. Antoinette has told me and a multitude of people that she counsels…"they will keep you from life itself." God's Holy Spirit freed her. Today, we share authenticity and growth and we both refuse to pick our masks up—ever again!

God has touched me miraculously through this astounding woman, Antoinette. She and the pages of this book have ministered strength to me and demonstrated her power to bounce back time and time again. In her case, what you see is what you get…but, it hasn't been a cake walk! Use her example to empower yourself and find a new way to walk in this world…FREE! The best you is yet to come!

Throughout all my efforts to change myself and help others to improve self-image, this has been the single most effect means, outside of God's Word itself, to gain hope and help. Real wisdom, real life, real sorrow, real work and real change!

You now have the privilege to meet the "real" Antoinette. I enjoy the thought of your transformation and the impact that this book will have on your life.

Sondra L. Schneider, Personal Friend
Life Coach and Mentor of Women at Large
Gig Harbor, WA

Foreword

I formerly met Antoinette Jackson March 2010, while attending several prayer meetings at her home. I saw her previously at our church services at By His Word Christian Center, but if I spoke to her at all, it was only in passing. April 2010, Toni and I were two of the six attendees to a Woman's Advance in Sequim, Washington that was hosted by Marilyn Braxton. This was my first opportunity to talk with Antoinette on a personal one on one basis, and opportunity to know her more in depth, and to experience a small portion of God's anointing on her life. After the Woman's Advance ended and the issues of living our lives overwhelmed us, neither of us took the time to cultivate our newly formed sisterhood. God brought us together again in October 2015 and what a powerful reunion this has been. Antoinette is a committed powerhouse of prayer and she preaches and lives JESUS – The Word (John 1:1-4, 14). God is the one and only true God. He is the God of reconciliation (II Corinthians 5:17-19). Antoinette's life style exhibits a public display of being an ambassador for Christ. She has brought such encouragement to me as I take note and learn from her example of faith, hope, joy and power in JESUS

Do you need JESUS to fill your emptiness? Take a walk with Antoinette through her life journey as you read "Taking off the Mask." Experience God's redemption, God's mercy, and God's grace as you read of her life journey. The same redemption, the same mercy and the same grace is available to you as you live your life in JESUS. Lean on the everlasting arms of JESUS. He gave His life for the world. Receive JESUS and trust in Him. He will fill your empty cup and give you beauty for ashes.

Thank you Minister Antoinette Denise Jackson - Mighty Woman of God, Defender of Truth in the Great Pacific Northwest.

Roselyn C. Knox
Tacoma, WA

I would like to start by telling you who I am today. I am Antoinette Denise Jackson, born in New Orleans, LA to Barry James and Marion Victoria on March 26, 1960.

I am saved and created to be like Christ.

I am born of God, I am complete in HIM.

I am informed and transformed by the knowledge of God.

I am renewed in the spirit of my mind.

I am a friend of Jesus.

I am a spirit being.

I am a new creature.

I am a joint heir with Christ.

I am an overcomer.

I am a believer Glory be to God.

"Taking off the mask!"

Now that you know who I am, today let's go back a little when I had no clue who I was.

When I was walking in fear, depression, abuse, isolation, anxiety, loneliness, no self-worth.

My story is not a blaming story, but one that I hope the readers can identify with and gain strength to move in a different direction.

I can remember my mask first being put on at the age of six while watching my mother being abused, being afraid and my brothers and I being told to keep our mouth shut. When she {my mother} had the strength to leave and make a better life for us, she was then a single parent working and going to school to be a nurse. We needed child care and that's where life went sour for me because the babysitter's son raped me. The babysitter had a doctor appointment and asked her 22 year old son to watch the 4 children in her care until she returned back home. While I was napping, her son woke me from my nap and told me to get in the room and make up the bed. Then, he began kissing on my face. As I tried to stop him, I was yelling and hitting him which made him angry. He yelled at me to shut up. Then, he started to pull my pink shorts down and began licking me on my private area. I was crying and scared, hoping someone would come into the room. Next, he raped me. There was blood everywhere. It was violent. Afterward, I sat on the bedroom floor crying and I was in excruciating pain. He tried to clean up the mess, but at this time the babysitter came in and asked, "What's going on?" She found me. I was badly injured and needed medical care. They couldn't hide it. My mother was called and I was rushed to the hospital and stitched from front to back. Yes, I was six years old and I was raped. Her son was arrested and the babysitter blamed me. As a child you don't understand being told it's your fault doesn't make it easy to trust adults at all. Now my mom had to make a decision and of course she removed my brothers and myself from this home. Good choice, but now we had another dilemma, mother had to teach us how to be home alone until she could find another sitter. She still had to work and go to school to make a living for our family. I had to learn some basic things to keep me and my two brothers safe and cared for. Cooking, cleaning, making sure homework was done, baths, and bedtime, was the new charge for each day. My mother would say don't open the door for anyone not even JESUS, he has a key! Never tell anyone you are home alone. We ate a lot of sandwiches and I cooked a lot of grits, eggs, and canned soup. When mom was off we got red beans and rice, chicken you know the good stuff maybe even a family day out to the movies. My mother did eventually find another sitter about six months later. Ms. Gustavia and Grandpa Sam were an old couple in the City of New Orleans. They were very good to my brothers and I. We stayed in their care for five years then, Grandpa Sam went to be with Lord and Ms. Gustavia's health began failing. So now am 12 years old and my mother reached out to my biological grandmother for help. I can't recall who kept my brothers, but my grandma kept me for a while. About a year later, I met my father for the first time. It was good for a while, but then he went to jail for theft. We never had a father and daughter relationship. He wanted to be my friend, not my parent. So we got along for a while, he never spoke words of encouragement to me. Never taught me values, never said don't do this or that, never took me out for dinner or pulled a chair out for me. No father and daughter dance for me. He thought every time he showed up with a gift that meant he loved me. When I was about 15 years old, I remember asking him for money, (the one and only time) and his response was go sell your "good stuff" and make money. As a woman you should never be broke. So I needed to separate myself from him for a while. My grandma and I remained close until she went home to be with the Lord. The next man I thought would be important in my life would be my mother's father, my grandfather. He was a Baptist preacher, we were always in the church at this time, but didn't learn much spiritually. Oh, he could hoop and holla and sweat, but there was no all-night prayer, no speaking in tongues, no change and a lot of cheating. I loved this man so much he was my bucket of sunshine, but carnal as the day is long. Well, then I didn't understand carnality so you did what you were told to do as a child. Kids see and hear things they shouldn't and then are told, "do what I say not what I do." (WHAT!) So I would sing when I was in pain or heard things I didn't understand. Music always took me to a happy place. So from 6 years old until today, I would just sing. I sing when am happy. I sing when sad. I sing when I need to make decisions and when things are on my mind—I just sing. My mother would have home bible study with us and our friends. We learned the Our Father prayer and the 23rd Psalm the Beatitudes and memorized the books of the Bible. But everybody was sleeping with everybody in church from pulpit to the back door. Just living out of the flesh, not the spirit. We were just adapting to our surroundings.

{NIV} John 6:63

The Spirit gives life; the flesh counts for nothing. The words I have spoken to you they are full of the Spirit and life.

{NKJV} Romans 8:5-8

For those who live according to the flesh set their minds on the things of the flesh, but those who live according to the Spirit, the things of the Spirit. For to be carnally minded is death, but to be spiritually minded is life and peace. Because the carnal mind is enmity against God; for it is not subject to the law of God, nor indeed can be. So then, those who are in the flesh cannot please God.

So, this is how we lived and how I was taught. So, "not much victory was going on." Just getting up getting dressed, going to church and full of pain and no change. Even when we made a mistake it was said, "Oh, God knows and He will forgive." It felt as if you could do whatever you wanted to do and just ask for forgiveness. I'm not saying my family wasn't saved, just that most didn't activate their salvation. They believed God/Jesus/ Holy Spirit to do all the work not knowing that being saved was Jesus' part and salvation is our part.

Philippians 2:12 says

Work out your OWN salvation with fear and trembling. {NKJV}

This brings me to my next turn in life, my first year of high school and dating. I was pregnant at sixteen with my first son. My mother was always working and there was no father in the home so I played house. I thought I was in love when in fact, I was immature, unhappy and made bad choices. Now, I was much too young to know all that love entails. The father of the child and I couldn't make the decision to parent the child. We were in need of being parented ourselves. We were both in school in Raceland LA. We were scared, but supported each other best we could. My son's grandmother on the father side did all she could to make life easy for us, but my mother blocked every door. I remained in school and it was there that I met my very first, real girlfriend, Sharlene Reed. She supported me. She spent time with me and spoke the Word of God encouraging me to never give up. She would make tops for me to wear when my belly got big. She gave the baby shower for me and invited her friends and family to come.

She has done things for me that I could never pay back. We have shared homes together, tears together and yes, good times together. When I had nothing and no money and didn't want to call home out of embarrassment, she took care of me. I remember her selling her washer and dryer, furniture, household goods, to get enough money together to help me and my children relocate. Forty two years later, I have never heard one word about anything that she has done for me. She just loved me with an unconditional love. She saw a need and met it—over and over again.

Hebrews 13:16
Do not neglect to do good and to share what you have, for such sacrifices are pleasing to God. (ESV)

She was doing the Word and I have learned so much from her. I pray always that every one of her needs will be met. I love you always, Sharlene. Thanks for everything!

Matthew 6: 4
So that your giving may be in secret. Then your Father, who sees what is done in secret, will reward you. (NIV)

My baby, Chad Lamont was born January 13th, 1976. He was 6 lbs. 11 oz. Thanks Sharlene for then and now. My mother's way to deal with this was to pack up and move the family to another state, which means my mother would have to care for me, my two brothers and my child. We never talked about it, never asked father of the child what part he or his family wanted to play. She just told me what was going to be. And that hurt worse than becoming pregnant. I know my mother meant well and you can't give what you don't have. I know that now, but then I felt like I had a disease and she didn't want me around. She didn't want anyone to see her as a failure. I think she felt guilty and bad for having to work and leave us alone. We never had the kind of relationship where we could talk about anything. My mother had her own mask to deal with. She was an awesome grandmother and did all she could to help me. My mother, auntie and eight children loaded up the U-Haul and the car and moved the family to Pasadena, California. But, on the other side, my son's father was hurting and wanted to be a part of raising his son. After a year and a half I reconnected my son and his father. We kept in touch through letters and phone calls and for that am grateful.

Plans were made and new housing was set up. My mother was a nurse so employment was not hard for her to get. I went back to school and put my son in day care. Things were going well. Everyone around me seemed to be happy, but I was still in pain on the inside. I was still missing my son's father, but doing what was expected of me. My baby was growing up and starting to walk and say little words like, "mama" and "Toni" but he was calling my mother, "mama" and calling me, Toni. I didn't like that very much at all. My mother don't see anything wrong with it. I needed to do something. My oldest cousin and I became close and I was able to open up with him and talk about the things that was bothering me. He heard me and gave me a safe place to be myself. He listen and we decided to get a place together. Now I just needed to convince my mother it was a good thing to do. My mother and I had the talk and she agreed to let me move in with my cousin since he was family she too felt that I would be safe. So, she gave her blessing and help me to set up my bedroom with things that Chad and I would need. Being on my own felt good, even though my mother was right in the same apartment complex, I had a sense of being independent. My cousin and I did well together our bills were paid. We had food in the house and he even help me with the care of my son. One evening, my cousin came home with a friend. I needed a bookcase moved from my mother's house to mine and the friend was willing to help. So, you know what happen. We became close. He started coming over spending time with me and taking time with my son. He was very kind and polite and never tried anything sexual with me. We would talk about our family issues with each other. After about six months, we started making plans to be together. This young man decided to go into the Marines and get through basic training and if he could get through it, he would return and I would become his wife. For 3 months we talked on the phone, wrote letters and encouraged each other to stay focused. In the mean while my mother moved to (Watts) in Los Angeles to be closer to her job. She was a nurse at Martin Luther King hospital. Chad and I moved back home with her. Now my new boyfriend has returned from basic training and he passed with high honors and received a BIG bonus. When he got back he asked my mom for my hand in marriage. At 17 years old, I was to be a bride. I needed my mother's permission. I wasn't old enough to sign the paper work myself. My mother did sign and gave her permission. Why? I really don't know. I think sometimes because she wanted something or someone for me or maybe she was just tired of feeling responsible. Never the less, I had myself a Marine, a smart man, a kind man, a loving man, a provider. Now I was making new plans to be married and move to a new home. Are you thinking, where is Jesus in all this? Well, He's around I'm just not spending as much time with Him as I should and I'm trying to replace one thing with another. You know how that goes. But the word works whether we do it or not!

Romans 8:13
for if you live according to the flesh, you will die; but if by the Spirit you put to death the misdeeds of the body, you will live. (NIV)

So even though things seemed well for me, my husband treated me well and life was feeling pretty good. As you can see, Jesus was left out of the decision making process which means TROUBLE. We were married June of 1977, in Los Angles, California. We had a wonderful reception at my new husband's family's home in Pasadena. We received a honeymoon gift of an overnight stay in a really nice hotel. My husband had to report for duty in two days so we packed what little we had and got on a greyhound bus and moved to Oceanside, California. Because of that BIG bonus we were able to get an apartment off base and pay rent ahead for six months. Oh yeah, I got pregnant on our honeymoon with my second child. It was the first time we had been together.

So now we're all moved in, my husband has checked in for duty and making friends. We went to a second hand store and got a bed, sofa, table and chairs and a few other things needed to make our house a home. We had the weekend alone in our home to settle in and just enjoy all that just happened. Monday morning came and hubby had to go to work. I am home being a good wife by cooking, cleaning, being mama and enjoying marriage. After about a month my husband suggested I meet some of his Marine friends' wives, so I tried to be social with a few of them. I became close with one young lady. Now when he was working I had someone to spend time with, go shopping with. Take my son to the park with. Missing my mom a little but wanting things to work with my new family, I just kept quiet.

After 3 months of marriage…something happened. Oh no, "What have we done." "Who can I call?" I am in this place with no family-no friends. I need someone NOW! What should I do? We were trying to be grown and was running from home. Trying to prove we can do this marriage thing. Of course we thought anything would be better than what we had. NOT!!!! Everything that could go wrong did. "We are young and naive and being taken advantage of. My husband was introduced to drugs by his new friends which caused him to act differently. The friends then took it upon themselves to take advantage of me. They had a plan and it wasn't for good.

They tied me to the bed for days. "Oh no! What about my baby? Oh no, not my baby." They put my son in the bathroom with ice cream and Spanish fly to drink. "Why are they raping me and where is my husband?" Over and over and over again "it" keeps happening. Should I give up? No, my baby is in the bathroom, I have to fight. But I feel like dying. I feel helpless. I feel hopeless. "What are they going to do to us next?" "God, please don't let them kill me, my baby, my husband and unborn child. "I want my mama!" "Oh no, I don't even have a phone." They will be leaving soon they have to return to work. It will be over soon. I can do this. They left me tied to the bed and threaten me to keep my mouth shut or they would be back to "take care of us."

"They are gone now." I called for my husband he's coming around, but he's acting different. He untied my legs and wrist and I was able to get my baby out of that bathroom and clean him up and the mess. Am pregnant haven't been to a doctor yet. I had no money and had to depend on my husband for everything. I wanted to go home I needed my mom so I asked my husband if we could call her just to say hi and let her know we were ok. I just wanted her to hear my voice, he said he would call at the pay phone. So, he called her and told her that I was home taking care of the baby and the house and he was out running errands and decided to give her a call and let you know we are doing well. My mother asked a few question and told him to tell me hello that she missed me and call soon and give baby boy a big kiss. While he was gone I just cried out "Lord help me, please get me and my baby out of this situation." My husband called into work and took a few days off to get himself together. This was in September coming up on his birthday when his Nana would come to celebrate with him. Now I had a plan. She's a woman, maybe she would help me? The day she came we had good food, a nice cake, music, laughter. Then she asked my husband to go to the store for her. He was having such a good time and happy to see his Nana, he was glad to do whatever she asked. While he was gone I said, "Nana may I please talk to you?" She said. "Of course." I said, "I need help." Something bad has happen and I want to go home. I showed her the ropes and ask her to at least call my mother and tell her to come get me. Nana said, "Baby, I don't want to get involved in anything, but take this 15 dollars and if anything happens again leave." I said, "thank you and can you keep this between you and I, please don't say anything to my husband." She agreed not to say a word so my husband returns from the store. We talk another hour or so then we called a cab for Nana to leave. My husband and I walked out to wait with Nana and she turned to him and said, She told me and I gave her a few dollars to go see her mother if it ever happens again." (WHAT!!!) Didn't I say keep your mouth shut?!?! He grabs my arm like he's hugging me and whispers in my ear, "what did you say." Then he smiles at Nana and said, "Oh Nana, I love her I wouldn't hurt her." I'm thinking...I'm about to die. He did hit me that night. I just tighten my body up so it won't hurt so badly and thank God he didn't hurt my baby. I am 3 months along and 75lbs. He wanted the money she gave me and thank God I put it away before he came from the store. She gave me a 10 dollar bill and a 5 dollar bill. I put the 5 in my bra and the 10, well I used it like a tampon. He made me strip all clothes off he found the 5 dollars and never look for more. At that time it was only $4.80 to ride a greyhound bus from Oceanside to Los Angeles. So, he was satisfied. My mind was racing over what to do. I need to get me and baby out of here. I cooked a nice meal, washed laundry and cleaned house. I just went along like everything was okay. But now he don't know what's going on in my head. We went to bed, slept together next morning he asked me to go to phone booth to call his job and tell them he was under the weather and wouldn't be in. YES!!!...my way out! Now, I just needed to make sure baby boy goes with me. I got dress, headed for the door knowing my son was scared of him. He began to cry which bothered my husband so he said, "take that crying baby with you." "YES! YES! Thank you Lord it is working." I took my baby a bottle of milk, my 10 dollars and "**we were OUT**!!!!!!!!!"

He did throw a glass of alcohol on me before I went out of the door. I didn't care. I was out! I cried all the way to bus station. People thought I was drunk because of the smell of alcohol on my clothes and am sure I looked a mess. My feet and back were hurting, but I was not going back. I was so scared he was going to come looking for us. It took a while to walk to bus station. When I arrived, I went in the bathroom removed my 10 dollars, washed it and put it under blow dryer. I took care of my baby. I washed his little face made sure he had milk and a snack with the change we had after purchasing the ticket. I then called my Auntie, "the next rock in my life." My ride or die. I love her so much and I let her know all that happened and she said. "Come on home." My mother was out of town at the time. We got on that bus and when the doors close and we took off. I cried so hard for so long, "thank you Jesus am free, am free." I needed Jesus. I called on him and he answered.

Jeremiah 29:12
> *Then shall ye call upon me, and ye shall go and pray*
> *unto me, and I will hearken unto you. (NIV)*

Now, I am at the point where I arrived in Los Angeles and Chad and I took the city bus to my Auntie's house. I was weak and hungry and my baby was wet. I was so glad to see my Auntie! It was about 6 PM, when the phone rang and it was my husband. He asked my Aunt had she seen me because I had went out earlier to use the phone and didn't return. And of course, she said, "NO," as I arrived weighing 75 lbs. and traumatized. Later that night, he called again, I answered the phone. He said something really bad had happened and he needed help. I asked, "What kind of help?" He said that he needed money sent by Western Union. He had killed the apartment manager. (He snapped and stabbed the man to death.) I told him that I would send the money to Western Union and when he went to pick it up, he was arrested, tried and served 37 years in San Quintin Penitentiary. (He was released December of 2016. At the time of this writing he and his son have not met face to face, however, they have had a telephone relationship over these years.)

I was now residing with my mother (again) and my Auntie. I was receiving treatment for my prenatal care AND for my psychiatric needs. (They were afraid that I was going to "Nut Up!")

I could hear the therapist, at one of my appointments, tell my mother, "Maybe my mother needed to put the children/her grandchildren in her name. I became afraid of losing my kids and they were my reason to live. I took some control of things and moved with my son to the "back house" to begin my own recovery and reconnect with God. I attend church with my mother and I began to feel better about myself and felt stronger.

Psalm 107:19-20

> *"Then they cry unto the Lord in their trouble, and he saveth them out of their distresses. He sent his word, and healed them, and delivered them from their destructions." (NIV)*

I began feeling safe and secure in myself, but I was still isolating myself keeping others at arms distance out of fear of being hurt. I hadn't shared my pains with anyone. Only my Auntie and my mother peeked under my mask.

Learning to trust in God to take me through my troubles, I was starting my true journey of faith. I was getting to know God for myself, not because of my mother's faith, but because of my own faith in God. Like it says in

Hebrews 11:1
"Now faith is the substance of things hoped for, the evidence of things not seen." (KJV)

Now my hope is in what Jesus has already done for ME!

Life for me was taking shape. I was back in school, but this time it was a school for pregnant teens and teen mothers called, Sojourner Truth High School. I loved that school. I met one of my best friends there. Her name was Alma. Alma and I opened up to each other. She was the first person in Los Angeles that totally accepted me. She knew my faults and failures and hurts. She never rejected me or judged me. We are still friends today—41 years strong!

Six months later and I'm having pains. I think it's time! So, what I'll do is clean the house, do the laundry, take a nice bath, put on a gown and called an ambulance. Then, I called the front house to ask them to watch Chad, because "Baby #2 is on the way!" I arrived at the hospital and I was there about 3 hours. The staff sent me home and said, "Not yet." Hum, castor oil! Yes, that's what I'll do. I drink a 6oz bottle and about 45 minutes it kicked in and everything started to come out so I called the ambulance again. This time upon arrival they said I was ready. They found that the cord was wrapped around his neck, so I had to have an emergency C-Section. He had complications. His first stool went into his lungs and his coloring was purple. I couldn't see him for the first 3 days of his life. The doctors withheld him from me for fear that I would panic at his condition. I named him Andre Joseph born April 14, 1978 and he was 7 lbs. and 11 oz., my "Middle Man." We finally made it to our cozy little home together and settled in.

We churched it up for two years, my two sweethearts and I. However, one Saturday evening, I was sitting on porch at the big house waiting to go to church that evening. A "Teddy Pendergrass" came walking up. I was looking down and I heard a deep voice say, "Hello, young lady." I raised my head and said, "Hi." He made small talk of course and asked if I was going somewhere. I replied, "Yes, to church." He said, "May I go with you?" and I said, "Sure!" So, the kids and I rode with my mom and this tall drink of water followed behind in his sky blue caddy with a white landau top. After church, he asked if he could drop me off at home. I agreed for me and the boys to accept his offer. He stayed and we sat outside and visited and told me about himself. He was a professional basketball player. He played a little with the Lakers and the Utah Jazz. After his basketball career, he worked for General Motors and for another Detroit based company which moved him to LA. His family lived next door to my mother. In time, I didn't resist so much. We shared life, ourselves and a baby was made. It felt good to have someone care, but I didn't trust my own instincts or him totally. I had become a master of criticizing myself, beating myself up and hemorrhaging internally. He wanted to marry me, but the fear of where I had come from paralyzed me. What he wanted didn't matter because I couldn't trust myself yet to make good choices concerning men. He asked me to go with him and be a family, but I rejected him. I couldn't trust that deeply to uproot my children and myself. I was afraid of going so far away. I was so satisfied with my gains and the rebuilding of my faith that moving away could put me back in jeopardy. I would know— not a soul in Michigan. Eventually, he moved back to Michigan and I was pregnant and alone once more.

We kept in touch and when James Darnell was born on September 17, 1980 at 8 lbs. 11 oz. I notified him and was given one more opportunity to be wed and move to Michigan. I couldn't bring myself to put my life in another man's hands. Remember, I've come from A.B.U.S.E. Abusive relationships having a cracked skull, broken ribs, moving my babies from one town to another and living in women's shelters, not to mention sexual rape—ENOUGH IS ENOUGH! Keeping this mask on was painful and it effected everybody in my life.

At night, I would comfort myself by singing to myself and it works! Try it:

> My hope is built on nothing less, than Jesus'
> blood and righteousness.
> I dare not trust the sweetest frame, but wholly

lean on Jesus name.

We moved on. The best gift that he gave me was our baby boy, "BJ" for baby James. He got married within a year and I diapered babies and continued to work on my healing through the Word of God. I started with Psalms and Proverbs. I found that GOD LOVES ME! No Matter What!!! AND HE CARES!

Psalm 118:6
> *"The Lord is on my side; I will not fear, 'What can man do to me.?' (ESV)*

Out of this love, I opened my mouth unto the Lord and sing. I sang in church choirs and school choirs. My mother and I sung together in Mother/Daughter concerts. Our favorite song together was "Leaning On The Everlasting Arms."

The lyrics ministered more to me than anyone in our audiences.

What a fellowship, what a joy divine, leaning on the everlasting arms;

When Chad was 6, Andre was 4 and James was 2, I made a decision to step out on my own from under my mother's wings. I returned back to my old home, New Orleans. Sharlene was there and we lived together for a short time until I got my own place. I reconnect Chad with his dad and he helped in raising his son. Chad lived with this dad every other year until he was a preteen. Then he stayed with me until he was fully grown.

The years in New Orleans began to feel empty and I desired more. I didn't feel like I was being fed spiritually. The Church hadn't change and I had and I needed more in order to raise my kids differently. So, I had a talk with Sharlene about wanting to go somewhere that I've never been. Since I still communicated with James' father, I decided to try Michigan. In order to do this, I needed money, a ride, a place to go and Sharlene stepped up to help us. This is when she sold her own things, dropped everything and made it happen. We drove from New Orleans to Flint and I began a new life.

With the help of James' grandfather, a home was waiting for us. He provided me with a two bedroom house. Sharlene helped me unpack and saw that we had what we needed before she left. The next time that I saw Sharlene she was a mother of two and it had been about 5 years, but I always knew she was "there for me."

My years in Michigan were from 1985-1991. I was filled with the Holy Spirit at Pentecostal Compassion (COGIC) Church of God in Christ. The boys flourished also. We were all happy and healthy. We stayed in that home and grew and healed. I was licensed in Ministry in 1989, thru Lighthouse of Prayer and Pastor Edward Fleming's.

Drenching myself in the Lord, I refreshed my soul. I still couldn't process my guilt and shame. I began to "numb-out" my feelings. To trust meant to become vulnerable and to give myself permission to make mistakes was still too scary.

I had to learn the difference between good and bad fear. I know that bad fear hates change, does not want to heal and is not willing to trust anything or anyone.

John 10:10,
> "The thief cometh not, but that he may steal, kill and destroy. (KJV)

And good fear;

2 Timothy 1:7,
> "God has not given us the spirit of fear, but power, love and self-discipline." (KJV)

2 Corinthians 5:17,
> "Therefore, if anyone is in Christ, he is a new creation. Old things have passed away and behold, all things have become new." (KJV)

I had to learn a new way of thinking, being and doing. I had to renew my mind.

Romans 12:2,
> "Don't copy the behavior and customs of this world, but let God transform you into a new person by changing the way that you think. Then you will know God's will for you which is good pleasing and perfect." (NLT)

I took the advice and wisdom of the church mothers that you have probably heard them say, "Find a man in the church!" So, while singing my heart out, I met the music minister. I directed the choir, he played the piano and we formed a gospel group. Before long, we found ourselves wanting to know each other more. Since I had gained such confidence, I decide that I would reach out and invite him to a home cooked meal. He was accepting. We really hit it off.

This is where you should be led of the spirit and walk in the spirit. We should not assume that the church people are without question. I didn't question enough. I found after marriage that he was an alcoholic and drug user. I remained with him for 11 years. He was a provider, but a functioning drunk and when my mother suddenly became blind due to diabetes, our family moved quickly to Tacoma, WA. I was the oldest child and only girl of my mother and she needed me. My relationship to my husband suffered more after the move, but, I didn't see adultery coming. I endured a few affairs trying to uphold the image of a faithful wife and a Christian and not wanting to expose my husband. We were serving in our new church community while these secrets were mounting. After a phone call on my birthday from a "sister" and "friend" in Christ this life changed. She said that my husband had been having lunch and "other things" for the past year with her. She said that she needed to let me know because she loved me and didn't want to hurt me any longer. But I later found out that her real reason for telling me was because now he found a new love interest.

(Her daughter)

My mother had been teaching me to forgive because I was a Christian and I had to follow Jesus' example. I got a locksmith and changed the locks on front and back door, packed his clothes into his truck. I parked it on the side of the road and went and filed for my divorce papers the next day, instead.

We didn't have children together. Our divorce was due to the drugs, which led to money problems, which led infidelity.

By this time I was strong enough in the Lord to know that I had a helper that would teach me all things. He would guide me and comfort me.

John 16:13,

"Howbeit when He, the Spirit of Truth, is come, He will guide you in all truth: for He shall not speak of himself but, whatsoever, He shall hear, that shall He speak, and He will show you things to come." (KJV)

I knew I didn't want the old ways, —looking alright, but not being alright. It's time for me to go inside and deal with the hard stuff.

John 15:7,

"But if you remain in me and my words remain in you, you may ask anything you want and it will be granted." (NLT)

I had to learn to listen inwardly rather than outwardly. Outwardly, I had learned to trust what I see, hear, touch, taste and smell, but inwardly I had to change. I had to trust my heart, my new inward man. I had to give myself over to the still small voice that knows more than senses could ever reveal. So, how do I change and renew my mind? The word says,

Joshua 1:8
"Study this book of instruction continually. Meditate on it day and night so you will be sure to obey everything written in it. Only then will you prosper and succeed in all you do." (NLT)

I'm working on myself I needed to do the hard things that didn't feel good, but worked for my good. I couldn't let others manipulate me anymore, hurt me, use me on purpose-not even in the name of family or friend. So, I had to cut some relationships off. It wasn't easy because I was a people pleaser—making everyone happy at the cost of being unhappy. I had to trust God or go back. Going back wasn't an option because I would die.

Proverbs 3:5-6
"Trust in the Lord with all your heart, do not lean on your own understanding. In all your ways acknowledge Him, and He will make straight your paths. {KJV}

I'm starting to take off my mask, but taking it off and standing in my truth is feeling a little lonely. Everyone around me does not want to come in the light with me.

John 3:20

"Everyone who does evil hates the light and will not come into the light for fear that their deeds will be exposed." (NIV)

The healing that was taking place in me at this time was so awesome that all I could do was stand and follow His word.

Ephesians 6:13

"Wherefore taking unto you the whole armor of God, that yea may be able to withstand in the evil day and having done all to stand." (KJV)

In 1992, I am doing well. I got a nice three bedroom home in Spanaway, Washington. I became a foster parent in the Pierce County area. I have had 30 or more children come through my home. Their ages ranges from 10 days old to 18 years old. One of the young ladies I got at 14 years of age, later became the mother to my oldest grandchild. (Oops!) Guess you know what happened. Yes, she and my middle son decided to play house and of course, I didn't find out until later. In January on the 23rd 1996 a baby boy was born. I still didn't know he was my grandson for another year.

By October of 1995, tragedy hit my home. My middle son and four of his friend were out for Halloween and robbed some homes and they were caught and arrested and found guilty of the crimes. Charged as adults, my son was sent to Walla Walla State Penitentiary to serve a 12 year sentence.

I thought I would just die. I was all for him paying for what he had done, but it didn't make the pain any easier to bear. The church treated me differently; no support, no love, no invites, no prayers. Everything just stopped. I was treated as if I committed the crime myself. It was all over the news, in every paper, when I went to the stores people would point at me. It was devastating. One evening, I was doing a young lady's hair and she reached out to me and ask would I like to get out of the house for a little while and go listen to some jazz. I drove so if they wanted to drink I would be the designated driver. She was my Good Samaritan for the church had cross the street.

Read Luke 10:25-37.

We went to Pioneer Square in Seattle, Washington to a club called Larry's where different bands took turns playing a set.

One of the young men that sung that night noticed me sitting alone in the back of the club reading a book. He came and introduced himself to me and asked if he could sit with me. I didn't mind because I was hurting so badly I didn't really care. He said you sure look out of place in here. Do you come often? I said no it's my first time. He started a conversation about a book he was reading. What I found intriguing about him was that he said he would come every weekend to just sing. He didn't drink or smoke. He was in college and co-parenting his 3 year old son. Had a book to read sat in the back of the club and went to the stage when he was called. At the end of the evening he walked us ladies to my car and gave me his number and said he would love to hear from me sometime. After a few days of going to court, listening to the trail with my son, I just needed a break so I decided to call him. I am feeling pretty bad and I don't feel that I could call the church, so I reached out to him. In tears on the phone, he ask would you like to just get away for a few hours. I can cook you dinner and be a listening ear. I accepted the offer and went. Dinner was amazing and he let me just talk and cry and talk some more. After a while he was going with me to see my son in prison and doing nice things for me. We began spending more time together. I met his mom and kids and he met my kids. We began dating and we were married in June of 1998. Now, I did ask about his relationship with Lord and he said he knew him, but wasn't active in a church. Since I wasn't either at this time because of my pain, I thought okay we can do this at home alone. Well, you know that doesn't work for the word says in

Psalm 92:13
> *Those that be planted in the house of the Lord shall flourish in the courts of our God. {KJV}*

I knew that we wouldn't make it trying to be an island unto ourselves. I knew where I had come from and the consequence of leaving Jesus out of my decision making. I began visiting other churches until I found one that worked for my family. After a few months of searching I did find a good church. It had strong leadership with a wonderful pastor and an active children's ministry. We started together as a couple, but I found myself going alone. After the first year, I went to the pastor for counseling, however, his recommendation was for me to end the relationship, because of some abuse and infidelity. At that time, I wasn't ready, I wanted my marriage to work. I had agree to support our family while he finished college for his Master's Program, but infidelity kept happening as well as abuse. I had to face the facts that I had made yet another mistake. It was time to cut the soul ties with this man. So, one day as he left to go to school, I rented a U-Haul and got an apartment about a mile away. I got a restraining order, filed for my own divorce, represented myself in court and won all within 90 days. My husband did give me biblical and every other grounds to divorce and I gave him his name back.

My boys, now grown men, wanted to defend their mom. Chad was ready, willing and able to come to my aid. I had to down play my hurts to protect them for engaging in retaliations.

He didn't go away quietly. He continued to harass me by calling, peeping in my windows and threating my life whenever he felt like it. I really couldn't put my trust in restraining orders. I think what kept him from hurting me badly was the feared of being separated from his son through going to prison.

The pressure that I was under from the divorce and other demands were too grave to share with my ailing mother. She had decided to relocate to New Orleans, Louisiana to be closer to her sister.

My life was changed yet again by a phone call from jail. It was my foster daughter asking me to pick up her kids from a hotel. She had been arrested and had abandoned them two days prior. However, I found that CPS had just taken the kids into custody. The hotel clerk informed me that my oldest grandson and his sister were with CPS, Child Protective Services. Being the biological grandmother, I was given the opportunity to take them into my home. While in my care, their mother lost her parental rights and the children were now put up for adoption. Because of my love for my grandson, I applied to be the adoptive parent of both children. I didn't want to separate them. We became a family in 2000. I changed their names to Jackson. He was 5 and she was 3 years old at that time. They continued to call me grandma, because that's who they knew me as. Within 6 months my grandson began displaying major behavior problems and my granddaughter was acting very withdrawn. I questioned what could be the cause so, I took them for a mental health evaluation. The specialists got him to talk and we learned that in their former foster placement my grandson was being sexually abused. We continued therapy however his behavior remained disruptive at school and he was taken from his mainstream classes into special education. My granddaughter schooling was not interrupted. She strived for acceptance and popularity, but struggled with peer pressure and low grades.

The next turn in our lives was the death of my father from cancer. The kids and I were southbound on a greyhound bus to spend three final days with him. When we arrived he could only speak one word, "potato." I wasn't leaving without making sure that he was saved. I said the sinner's prayer and asked him to blink if he understood. One for yes and two for no. I asked him, "Do you know Jesus?" He blinked once. I asked, "Would you like to say the sinner's prayer with me?" He blinked once. I began praying, "Lord Jesus, come into my heart…do you understand, Daddy?" He blinked once. I continued…"save me from my sins. I believe you died and rose again and I am saved." And he blinked once and began to cry and he said, "Potato."

I kissed him good-bye and returned home. One week later he passed away. It was November 8, 2002.

Now, my mother soon became very ill. I learned through a phone call that she was taken to the hospital. I had just buried my father 4 months prior. She was dying. Diabetes, congestive heart failure compounded with multiple strokes consumed her on March 28, 2003. One day after her birthday, she went home to be with the Lord. For years I carried the last photo of us. It was a photo of her on the phone, while in the hospital bed, attempting to speak to my brothers through her trichotomy port. This was their last phone call together and they were reassuring mother that it was okay to go. (My son Andre always teased me about carrying this in my wallet like a school picture.)

My mother's burial was on April 3, 2003, in New Orleans, Louisiana. She was 61 years old and I was 42. I still needed a mama. She is now with the Lord.

The pain and loss of my parents took a toll on my health. I was suffering from high blood pressure. I had been a diabetic for 15 years, but at this time became a Type II. Due to the stress of life challenges, I had a lumbar spinal stroke on Christmas Day. I began feeling tingling in my feet. Later that day it moved up my legs and body to my face. My face dropped and my speech was slurred. I drove myself to the hospital while brother watched the children. They informed me that it was a stroke and that I had to be admitted. I remained there for 3-4 days. Within the next year, every 3 months I was having TIAs or small strokes. This caused me to be effected from my neck all the way down my left side to this day. There were many activities that I could not perform. I needed a health care provider and rehabilitation. The sudden change of mobility and dependency on canes and walkers reduced my desire to be social and outgoing. I became depressed. Help for me came in the form of my care provider, Dody! My friend, she definitely was a big part of me living. She help me walk again, loved me unconditionally was very patient with me. Cooked meals for me and the kids. Kept my house immaculate. She did for me what I couldn't and treated me with integrity. I was housebound before receiving her care and isolated. I had stopped going to church because of my condition. It was a mega church and I wasn't even missed. I wanted to go back to church. I needed to hear the word. Faith come by hearing and was tired of TV church. I needed to be around people again. Dody heard my heart and took me to By His Word Christian Center of Tacoma, Washington. I was suffering inwardly over my disability and my grandson was taking advantage of my weakened condition as a teenager. He went too far. He ran away from home. He was exploited by two older men who enticed him with drugs and alcohol and sex. They began robbing, stealing and committing all types of crimes together until they got caught. My grandson was 16 years old and tried as an adult and sentenced to 30 years in the same penitentiary as his father, Walla Walla State Penitentiary. The men only received 2 years. My heart was broken AGAIN!

This time I ran to the church. I didn't leave. I was embraced. Good church, good pastor, good Word and eleven years later I have learned so much. I gained some physical strength back and also gained a lifetime friend in Dody. She loved me, she supported me, she would fight for me, she took care of me and she did this for 12 years. Our earthly bond was severed on February 25, 2015. She was always strong and we had a talk about her taking care of me as my health designate and holding my power of attorney. So, when I received the call at 2pm that she was in the hospital,

I was shocked. And at 5pm, I was informed that she was on life support. Her death has caused me to "GET UP and MOVING!" I'm motivated by the reminder that life is unpredictable and I'm taking better care of myself spiritually, mentally and physically. I miss Dody but I know for sure that we will see each other again, looking forward.

My church, By His Word, responded in love and protection. Prayer and support flooded me. My grandchildren and I were also given a safe place to develop our walk with the Lord. Time will hopefully mature those planted seeds in them.

Philippians 1:6

"Being confident of this that He who began a good work in you will carry it on to completion onto the day of Christ Jesus." NIV

"Let's Talk About Siblings"

I have two amazing brothers. Even when life was complicated we could come together without explanation and get it done. My brothers were my first friends and the first people that I argued with. We have had our fights in childhood, but now "at the end of the day" we LOVE each other, help each other, and take care of each other. We have learned to respect each other's space. My youngest brother and I talk daily and never hang up the phone without saying "I love you." We don't see our oldest brother as often or talk to him as much, but if he calls us we show up. What I know for sure is that they love me. And I have no doubt that they know I love them. "Sean, you are my superhero, you are busy and do have a life of your own, but nonetheless, whenever I need you for anything you surely are going to be there for me. Thank You! You are amazing I couldn't imagine life without."

"Jason, we have butted heads a few times, but when I need you or you need me just to listen we have been there for each other. I've been enjoying my once a month time with you. We have grown into awesome adults and I love you. We may not get together for every holiday or birthday, but we remind each other whenever we are together what's important. I pray that you draw closer to God and allow him to be your all and all." "Even in yawls' strength I see the sweetness and the tender side of you. When I am with either of you I feel safe and am grateful for God putting this family together? There were times when we couldn't protect each other and we would shut down, in our own way, as a result of how hurt we were by some of the things we were facing. I realize now that it has been hard for me to understand what you experienced as a man. We shut down in different ways and get up differently. You guys pretend not to care while I put on the happy face.

For me, growing up with two brothers has been precious. It has allowed me to better understand what some men and boys go through as they make their way in this world.

It is amazing to see you both today and feel who you really are without needing you to play a role or be tough or strong. I love that we can relax in each other company, as I allow myself to accept you exactly as you are and you accept me. As, I get older, I appreciate you both more." "Thanks Mom for everything you put in us and reminding us of the importance of family

"Hearing God Voice"

As I have grown in the Lord, I have really learned how to hear GOD's voice and have grown in the Spirit. It has been exciting and enriching. The closer that I have gotten to the Lord the thinner my crowd has become in the natural. Most of my phone calls are from people that need prayer, need a ride, need a meal and even sometimes need Jesus, but that's ministry. I have been blessed with good spiritual support. Not only am I reaching out to others, God has given me others to reach into me, to mentor me, speak in to my life and hold me accountable to the Word of God.

I'm learning how to even have positive relationships with the opposite sex and proper boundaries. I am learning how to forgive myself and others. I am learning that I shouldn't hold onto relationships that God has said" let go." In the past I've held onto relationships so tightly they have broken and were unrepairable. I'm learning to let go when I need to let go and hold tightly when necessary. Praying in the Holy Ghost has helped me in these areas and strengthened me more than you will ever know. It has changed my life!

THE HOLY SPIRIT
Jude 1:20

> *"But you, Beloved, building yourself up on your most holy faith, praying in the Holy Spirit." NKJV*

FORGIVENESS
Matthew 6:15

> *"But if you refuse to forgive others, your Father will not forgive your sins. NLT*

HEARING HIS VOICE
John 10:27

> *"My sheep hear my voice, and I know them, and they follow me." NKJV*

I had to learn to ask the question, "Is this you God?" The way I learned to recognize God's voice was to:

1. Test the origin. That's the place that it is coming from.

1 John 4:1

> *"Beloved, Do not believe every spirit, but test the spirits, whether they are of God; because many false prophets have gone out into the world." NKJV*

2. Compare what I'm hearing to the Word. Because God will never say something contrary to His Word.

1 Corinthians 2:13

"These things we also speak, not in words which man's wisdom teaches, but which the Holy Spirit teaches, comparing spiritual things with spiritual." NKJV

3. Compare the voice to God's nature.

1 John 1:5

"This is the message which we have heard from Him and declare to you, that God is light and in Him is no darkness at all." NKJV

Hebrew 13:8

"Jesus Christ is the same yesterday, today, and forever." NKJV

1 John 4:8

"He who does not love does not know God, for God is love." NKJV

4. Test the fruit. You are known by your fruit or how you act and your actions.

Matthew 7:15-20

Beware of false prophets who come to you in sheep's clothing, but inwardly they are ravenous wolves. You will know them by their fruits. Do men gather grapes from thorn bushes or figs from thistles? Even so, every good tree bears good fruit, but a bad tree bears bad fruit. A good tree cannot bear bad fruit, nor can a bad tree bear good fruit. Every tree that does not bear good fruit is cut down and thrown into the fire. Therefore by their fruits you will be know them. NKJV

5. Seek wise counsel.

Proverbs 11:14

"Where there is no counsel, the people fall; but in the multitude of counselors there is safety." NKJV

Toni & Sharlene

Toni & Dody

Ms. Nancy & Toni

Alma & Toni

Dody

Ms. Nancy

Friend

I have been truly blessed. It doesn't take many people to feel successful in friendship. One good friend is so important. Over the years and the many places that I have lived God has always provided me with friendship. In Washington, God brought me Ms. Nancy. We had our children in common. We worked together in life to cover each other with everyday needs. Whoever was paid first made sure the other had groceries, for example. We had the Lord and laughter between us. We never judged each other or questioned our relationship with God because of the choices that our children made. We remained friends over major tragedies. We both had children that were shot, incarnated, grandchildren born out of wedlock, infidelity, abuse and other painful burdens.

Proverbs 17:17
   "A friend loves at all times." NKJV

Remember Alma from Los Angeles, Sharlene from New Orleans and Dody from Tacoma? These were gifts from God to me! Some people never have even one good friend whom they can be authentic with, however, I've had several. In my bouquet of friendship, there are many wonderful women who have surrounded me with support, encouragement and correction. It is hard to write about the relationships that withered. As an example, I can admit that God gave me eyes to see that I was working to please and serve some of my associates for acceptance. The more I gave, for some, the more they took. Realizing that each person defines friendship differently, I had to decide to whom I should engage my time with and to whom I should give my heart. Some relationships are toxic. You know the kind. The kind that you leave feeling broken in spirit, inadequate, grieved, shot down, used, taken for granted and defeated.

1 Corinthians 15:33
> *"Do not be misled: Bad company corrupts good character." NIV*

Yes, God's Word is true! It doesn't always feel good, but it works for your good.

TO: MY BOYS
FROM: YOUR FIRST LOVE

When you boys were born you never came with instructions. I know I have made many mistakes along the way and for those I'm sorry. (Never was a prefect mom, but did the best I could with what I had.) I had a lot of baggage that I carried. Lack of understanding, lack of love in my relationships, abuse, and even not loving myself are a few examples of that baggage. That caused me to withdraw and hide behind a mask, which affected you boys. When I tell you I love you, I am not saying it out of habit, or as if it's the thing to do. I want you boys to know you're the best thing that ever happened to me. Many days you were my reason to get up and try again. I pray for you all always that you make the best of this life. I pray you be content in whatever state you're in. I pray you will forever be learning and growing in Christ Jesus. I pray you always will have shelter and a job. I pray God's peace be with you and God bless you with good friends.

CHAD "My Brave Warrior"

Psalm 28:7

The Lord is my strength and my shield; my heart trusted in Him, and I am helped: therefore my heart greatly rejoiceth; and with my song will I praise Him. {KJV}

There is something so significant in the relationship with your first born. We both have done a lot of "firsts" together and I often failed, yet we loved each other through them. It was with you my first little man that I learned unconditional love. No hidden motives, no expectation, just love. I studied you and you studied me. Now you're a man and I still know so little, but one thing am sure of we love each other. When we agree and when we don't see eye to eye we just love. Be good to yourself, be good to your children, and love the Lord God with all your heart soul and mind. Be proud of the things you do big or small.

Love you forever
MOM

ANDRE' "STRONG, MANLY"

Psalm 18:2

The Lord is my rock, and my fortress, and my deliverer; my God, my strength, in whom I will trust. {KJV}

My middle man! It was with you that I learned some hard lessons. I believe that in life we are never given any more than we can handle. We both had to learn to stand in adversity. Some may claim that life in the middle is hard, because you may feel forgotten, or overlooked. I pray that wasn't the case for you. When tragedy hit us, it was hard and devastating to stand apart in the natural, but together in the Spirit. Your strength help me to stand, to fight and to believe we would be okay. I see fire within you and I know you will make your way despite your place in the middle. You're a great dad and whatever your place in this family you are a perfect fit for me and I will always love you. MOM

JAMES "SUCCESSOR"

Psalm 18:35
You have given me the shield of your salvation, and your right hand upholds me, and your gentleness makes me great. {KJV}

My sweet baby James

I can hardly believe it's been 37 years since I welcomed you into this world. When I held you the first time my heart melted. A good and perfect gift from GOD. You are strong and smart and kind and intelligent. Most of all you love Jesus. You're a hard worker and of course, you married well. I'm so very proud of you. When I had you, my third child, my life was a mess. To be perfectly honest, I had no idea what I was doing. I had to learn right alone with you boys. I'm sorry that you were at the center of all my trails and errors. I hope you know my heart was always in the right place. I only wanted the best for you and still do. Despite myself, you turned out to be amazing. I'll love you forever, I'll like you for always, as long as I'm living, My Baby James you'll be.

"SIGNS OF HIDING BEHIND THE MASK"

- ANGER - Want just say I'm hurt
- Blame - Pointing fingers
- Avoidance - I'm fine, everything is ok
- Numbing - With alcohol, food, drugs, sex, shopping, perfection, gambling
- Isolation - fear of being known

Luke 8:17 [NIV]

> *For there is nothing hidden that will not be disclosed, and nothing concealed that will not be known or brought out into the open*

"Hiding Behind The Mask"

Behind every mask is a face and behind the face is a story and a performance. I hid behind my mask to feel confident, when I wasn't. I pretended to be calm, when I really wanted to exploded.

It allowed me to be happy when I was truly sad. I wore my mask everywhere; to church, to work, to dinner, with friends and in relationships. In some ways it made me feel safe. When people ask "How are you?" I thought, "Do you really want to know or is this just something people ask?" Like the sayings, "I love you." (What does that mean?) "Praying for you," ("REALLY!!")

Or "God bless you" ("Okay.") At first, I thought no one had a mask on, but me. NOT! As I grew in Christ and began praying with others, some allowing me the privilege of peeking behind their mask, I was amazed that I wasn't alone. I kept my emotions on lock down. Very few who knew me ever saw me cry. I did that alone. Wearing a mask all the time can be harmful and prevent you from developing genuine relationships. It is exhausting, maintaining a façade of "everything's okay," and "I'm fine, how are you?" Even when my mask was fastened on really tightly it was actually held on with fear and insecurity and doubt. God still sees all, knows all, and loves the real me.

Psalms 139:1-3, 13

O Lord, You have searched me and known me. You know my sitting down and my rising up; you understand my thought afar off. You comprehend my path and my lying down, and are acquainted with all my ways. For you formed my inward parts; you covered me in my mother's womb. NKVJ

I became a pleaser, ready to do anything for anyone to win approval. But, not too close to any. Some I allowed in and regretted it. I held in a lot of secrets and lots of scars. I learned never to reveal too much, because that would give someone power over me. If they really knew me would they like me? My fear of rejection was unbearable. So, I had a mask for church, a mask for work, a mask for friends, a mask for being a good wife and a mask for being a good mom. "Praise God today, I know that God has a plan for me."

Jeremiah 29:11

for I know the thoughts that I think toward you, says the Lord, thoughts of peace and not of evil, to give you a future and a hope. (NKJ)

His grace and love continues to be sufficient so that I don't have to feel like I need to wear this mask for the rest of my life. I forgive myself and I release all crippling quilt that I feel about the choices that I've made. I have learned not to get hung up on appearance.

1Samuel 16:7

But the Lord said to Samuel, "Do not look at his appearance or at his physical stature, because I have refused him. For the Lord does not see as man sees; for man looks at the outward appearance, but the Lord looks at the heart." {NKJV}

By sharing where I've been is not to glorify my past, but to bring glory to Christ for what he has done for me. I continue to grow and to learn as I come out from behind the mask. I pray you have been blessed and encouraged to take off your MASK and tell your truth risk rejection so someone else gets the courage to tell their truth.

Weather you have had pains or deep hurts like I have or you just needed a mask to face the world.

I will be praying for all of you that want to take the next step in taking off your mask.

Blessings (Toni)

Antoinette Jackson

"Food For Thought"

- Am I saved?
- Do I have the gift of tongues?
- Do I belong to a "good-Word" church?
- What am I grateful for _____.
- Name three people that are important in my life that I can be authentic with_____
- How often am I praying?
- Do I have faith in the Word?
- Do I confess the Word over myself and family?
- Am I a giver?
- Do I reach out in love to others?
- Do I have a good Christian mentor?
- How often do I read the Word?
- Do I know the different between Spirituality and Religion?
- Do I believe in Healing?
- Am I holding/hiding on to something or someone I should let go of?

- What do I believe in?
- Do I recognize God's voice?
- What I know for sure:

Prayer Of Salvation

God loves you-no matter who you are, no matter what your past.

Say the following prayer out loud and mean it from your heart.

Heavenly Father, I come to you admitting that I am a sinner. I choose to turn away from sin, and I ask you to cleanse me of all unrighteousness. I believe your son, Jesus, died on the cross to take away my sins. I believe that he rose again from the dead so that I might be forgiven and made righteous through faith in Him. Jesus be my Savior and Lord and fill me with the power of the Holy Spirit. I am free I am saved in Jesus name. Amen.

If you prayed this prayer, please contact me

Or send prayer request or for speaking engagements at tonijackson3@yahoo.com

"Take Off The Mask"

THERE IS A WALK THAT PEOPLE DO
EACH DAY
SOME WITH NOT KNOWING
SOME WALK NOT SHOWING
MANY WALK NOT EVEN GROWING
THERE IS A WALK THAT PEOPLE DO
CONTINUALLY THAT IS PRAYER
EACH AND EVERYDAY GOD MAKES
AWAY
EVEN WHEN WE HAVE GONE ASTRAY
COME TO HIM OUR LORD AND PRAY
HE IS THE ONE THAT WILL GUIDE
YOU
 AND HELP YOU
HE IS THE ONE THAT WILL DIRECT
YOU
ON THE WAYS YOU DON'T KNOW
 GOD CAN WORK WITH YOU

AS A NEW YOU BEGIN TO SHOW
BUT BEHIND YOUR SET OF EYES
THEY SHOW WHAT YOU FEEL
YOU MIGHT VOICE THINGS TO AP-
PEAR YOU'RE OKAY AND NOT BE REAL
I DO BELIEVE ALL THAT IS VOICED
SHOULD BE TRUE
YOU HAVE TO BE HONEST
BECAUSE GOD CAN HEAR YOU
NO NEED TO LIE
ALTHOUGH MANY PEOPLE DO
BUT IF YOU KNOW GOD HEARS YOU
LET GO OF WHAT HOLDS YOU
"BREAKFREE" LET GOD BE THE ONE
TO TALK TO YOU
LET HIS LOVE IN
WATCH HOW YOUR SITUATION
BEGIN TO FLOW
"BREAKFREE' PRAY TO GOD
HE WILL ALWAYS LET YOU IN THE
FAMILY
YOU WON'T BE BOUND NO LONGER
THERE ARE SO MANY EXPRESSIONS
THAT ONE FACE CAN HOLD
WHEN HE IS THE ONE
THAT CAN MAKE THE WEAK STRONG
NOT BEING HONEST FEELING LOST
WELL DON'T BECAUSE

JESUS PAID THE COST
SOME FIND IT EASY TO ESCAPE
HIDE IN PRIDE
FOREVER TRYING TO LIVE BRAVE
IT'S OK GIVE IT TO GOD
YOU DON'T HAVE TO STAY
ON A HARSH GRAVEL RIDE
IF YOU HAVE TO LEARN TO PRAY
BUT GOING ASTRAY IS NOT THE WAY
YOU DON'T HAVE TO SIT ALONE
IN A CIRCLE OR A BOXING RING
WHEN YOU REMOVE WHAT IS
HEAVEY
AND EXPOSE WHAT IS REAL
WATCH HOW GOD WORK
HE IS ABLE TO HEAL
TAKE WHAT YOU ARE GOING
THROUGH
THAT IS UNCOMFORTABLE FOR YOU
LET GOD LEAD YOU AND GUIDE YOU
WALK WITH YOU AND TALK WITH
YOU
LET GOD BE YOUR FRIEND
HE SAID THAT HE WOULD
NEVER FORSAKE YOU
AND YOU WILL BECOME BRAND NEW
TAKE OFF THE MASK
 BY: CARI SINGSON